And When I Dream:

Faces in San Francisco

Bert Katz

To Andre Anna & Ronnie —
Thank you for
buying the book!
all the very best!
Bert Katz

DayBue Publishing

DAYBUE PUBLISHING
Post Office Box 4961
Ketchum, ID 83340

First DayBue Publishing Edition 2002

DayBue Publishing, design, and logo are trademarks
of DayBue Publishing.

Book Design by Melton Eduardo Cartes

Printed in China

Library of Congress Catalog No. 2001096452

ISBN 0-9668940-4-9

To

San Francisco

And
The daughter who sailed the River Shannon, the Dartmouth grad
The sightless one who swims in winter
The man who'd walk barefoot
in the snow
And
the girl who stuck to the ceiling...the singing Muni driver...
the Jew who broke with 5,000 years of tradition
the doctor from Provincetown...the caregiver...
Romeo and Juliet in Germany...
the feisty Irishman and his Chinese bride

Also
The purple-spotted mountain hiker
The Yupi'k tribesman
The girl who never pays on the cable car
As well as
The Chinese girl who dances for Father God
And
Those who stopped just long enough to have their pictures taken
And
All the others

Words and Pictures

They came to San Francisco from all over the United States, Europe, Asia and the Americas. I would meet them on the street, in cafes, bookstores and in the workplace: The Muni bus driver who sings the Duke Ellington tunes all the way from the Castro to the Embarcadero, the personality kid who waits on us at the Bagdad Café, our Japanese friend who's never without his two dogs, my Chinese dentist who's married to an Irishman, the old Beat poet from Brooklyn who held forth in the Adobe Bookstore and scores of others over the years. We would arrange to get together another day, in their neighborhood or mine, and there we would walk around the block and take pictures in varying light and backgrounds. Next we'd sit on somebody's stoop or in a quiet café, where I'd turn my tape recorder on and they'd tell me about their lives. But for me, the best part came later, when I sat alone with the tapes and photographs and tried to understand these people. They were all smart, had a connection to the city and an abiding interest in family and loved ones, but, other than that, they didn't have much in common. Here in San Francisco we often speak of it as diversity. To illustrate this most cherished aspect of our city, I wish to document what lay in the hearts of a handful of individuals at this particular time in a very special American place.

Bert Katz

Acknowledgments

Grateful thanks to Melton Eduardo Cartes, Thalia King, Robert Jewkes, Kathy Zarur, Susan McGuire, Kashia, Liz Zivic, Val Hendrickson, Ebba Story, Marie-Paule Senavitis, Jeanne McGarraghy and Nancy Burke, Christina Burke, Elizabeth Day and Christopher Day of DayBue Publishing.

And When I Dream:

Faces in San Francisco

Bert Katz

Kelly

"I wore a mohawk back in the Eighties and had a tattoo on the side of my head. I was maybe the only funny-looking person in all of Minneapolis, which is where I grew up. I couldn't get a job the way I looked, so for two years I lived on the streets. Summers were no big deal. I could just climb up the side of a building and sleep on the roof. Or maybe I'd sack out under a bridge. Or in the boxcar of a train. One morning I woke up in Wisconsin. But it was rough in the winter, when the temperature fell to twenty degrees below zero. Sometimes, if I was lucky, I'd find an abandoned building and squat there 'til they tore it down. Or maybe I'd discover an old car somebody left behind and live in it for a few months. Or other times I'd walk the streets all night and just try to keep warm. I traveled everywhere in these United States to see what I could see. Including Chicago, which happens to be a really good place to meet weirdoes.

A buddy of mine was a janitor at the World Trade Center, one of the tallest buildings anyplace, and I freaked him out when I went up on the roof with him, hopped the guard rail and hung over the edge. The funny thing is I'm afraid of heights, always have been. It was really windy up there, too, and I was, like, shaking so hard... I do a lot of things that scare me...

I'd always heard that San Francisco is one of the weirdest places you can find, so that's why I came out here. The first time I went to Golden Gate Park to look for a place to stay, I realized, my God, there are thousands of people sleeping here. I'd wake up to stuff like cops ticketing me or somebody trying to mug me or Deadheads spare-changing me or calliope music and, once, to a big Krishna parade. A helluva sight for a kid from Minnesota.

No question, one of the best things about this city is the abundance of weirdoes. Where I come from they used to yell at me whenever I just walked down the street. Here I could paint myself with rainbow colors and go around buck-naked yelling stuff and nobody would notice. It's really nice being a weirdo and enjoying a sense of anonymity."

Liz

"My little sister and I wore hats and gloves and our prettiest dresses whenever we came into the city. Everybody got dressed up in those days – it was like going to church. And, with Mom driving, all it took was about fifteen minutes from our house in Corte Madera. Just through the tunnel, down the hill and across the Golden Gate Bridge.

My dad had a little store on Powell and Ellis and we'd visit. All the cable car guys would hang out there – the tracks ran right by the store – so my sister and I never had to pay. We'd just hop on the side and ride all the way down to Fisherman's Wharf and back. We'd eat Dad's candy, play with the cash register and wait on customers when he'd let us. They were mostly old people who lived in the downtown hotels and didn't have any families, so Dad would put their pictures on the walls and they'd become our family.

It felt like the whole city belonged to us. We'd walk through all the department stores, eat chocolate éclairs at Moar's family-style cafeteria and run down for lunch at the Emporium, where the waitresses were old and worked there all their lives. At Christmas time there'd be a big carnival on the roof, and we'd go up and ride the Ferris wheel and the roller coaster. Santa Claus would be there, too, and we'd get to pet his reindeer.

Dad walked with a cane – he'd been injured and captured on Wake Island, and he and my uncles spent the whole war in a prison camp – so he couldn't go on bike rides or hikes, but he and Mom always managed to take us places. We'd ride the carousel and the little boats in Golden Gate Park or go to the beach or fish in the lakes for rainbow trout. And sometimes it'd be just my little sister, me and Dad and he'd take us out to Candlestick Park. I always brought my baseball mitt along because I dreamed of catching a home run Willie Mays hit and getting him to sign it.

After college, I came here to live and work as a photographer. Mom's gone now, my sister lives in the Marina and Dad's eighty-five years old. I could've traveled around the world – could've settled in lots of interesting places – but I'm going to stay where I am."

4

Raoul

"I hear it's always been a haven for misfits like me, even as far back as 1849. A wild town, too. Twenty years ago, when I got here, you didn't need a lot of shekels for a groovy night on the town either. I'd start off the evening with a crab cocktail at Fisherman's Grotto on Pier Nine. Or maybe go up to Little Joe's in North Beach for the deep-fried calamari or a T-bone. Then I'd usually meet somebody interesting, have a couple of drinks, smoke a little weed and hit the sack. There'd be plenty of time in the morning for proper introductions.

Back in those days, there were seven women for every straight guy, and with those odds it was like shooting fish in a barrel with a spear gun. Which isn't to say there wasn't plenty of action for the ladies, too. Every year sailors from all over the world would come here with their little pom-poms on top of their hats. And all the girls from the Catholic schools would hurry down to Aquatic Park, Alioto's or DiMaggio's to meet them. The longshoremen would be getting off work and heading over to Red's Java House or the Eagle Tavern for boilermakers. And you could bet a Merchant Marine guy somewhere was fixing to stir things up with the Ecuadorian Navy.

When that Oregon Mist rolled in and blanketed the hills, it got so cold and dreary here everybody wore layers of clothes and scarves and sweaters. So in those days you'd sip an Irish coffee to offset the chill and look around the bookstores and laundromats for somebody to snuggle up with. One thing I always believed about this place – you don't take it seriously. I'd heard about all those famous rich people who came here – the Hearsts, Stanfords and Mark Hopkins – these guys weren't too tightly wrapped either. But they all knew how to have a good time. I often wondered: Why did they come here from Killarney, Tipperary and places all over the world? Was it because they just wanted to have something their mothers and fathers never had? Maybe they just wanted to get their yah-yahs up before the whole place went up in flames."

Katy

With graduation exercises finally over and our mothers standing there bawling their eyes out, we were, like, whatever – let's get on the road! So we packed up our friend's car, said our goodbyes, put on a Luscious Jackson tape and cruised out of town. Dartmouth had been a very white, very upper-class utopia and I was happy to be finished with it and driving cross country with my friends – playing our favorite music, smoking, staying overnight in cheap motels, taking pictures of random gas stations in the middle of nowhere and talking about the life we'd just left behind and all the stuff about to happen. I'd heard the most amazing things about San Francisco, how free, open and culturally exciting it was, like…there was a lot going on there. And, best of all, I'd be living with Brandon!

But, after four or five months of being together in San Francisco, Brandon and I became miserable around each other. He was having problems that were making me have problems. And I was doing things he wanted to do and not the things I wanted to do. And I couldn't figure out what I wanted to do because we were together all the time. But life is all about trial and error: If, for example, you go to some random poetry reading by someone you never heard of and the poet sucks that shouldn't stop you from listening to another poet. Just keep going and you'll hit on something.

And that's how I started living my life without Brandon, discovering what's out there. Going to clubs, listening to music and talking to all these people I've never seen before in my life. And, I'm, like, who's the next person who's gonna, like, really excite me? I went to this party in the desert Saturday night, and these people were, like, 'Oh, well, if you like this party then you should come to this other one.' It's all word of mouth, you know?

It's taken me awhile to get used to breaking up with Brandon. What we had was nice for a while, and the same with my other friends; it was easier having them around me in the beginning. But that's all over and it's about me now. I know that sounds selfish, but you can be selfish and considerate of people at the same time. I don't believe they're mutually exclusive. You can do the things that make you happy while caring for other people. Nobody wants to be responsible for your happiness, and you don't want to be responsible for theirs. That's too much pressure. When I first got here I didn't know how to get around, the things to do or how to interact . . . I stuck out like a sore thumb, like, here's this Boston girl and she obviously doesn't get San Francisco."

Heigo

"While I was growing up in Japan they pushed me to play with other children. It isn't the custom there to be alone. But I only wanted to be with my dog and play in the tall cedars near my village. Alone I could use my imagination, create exciting adventures and prevail single-handedly, no matter how difficult the circumstances. I dreamed I'd be king someday and make a peaceful revolution happen; I would end the group system forever and replace it with a society that celebrates the individual and his ability to perform by himself.

I used to read the history of my country and become disturbed when I saw how many wars we fought. Even soon after the tragedy of World War II, the fighting was still going on. Maybe not with airplanes and guns, but with economic weapons, used with just as much intensity and passion.

As a young man I put aside my dreams and studied to become an actor. A film company sent me to sword fighting school. But just as I was to appear in a film, I broke my leg while rescuing a dog. They put me in a hospital and I never returned to the acting profession again.

More and more, as the years passed, I watched Japan become a cultural copy of America. So, finally, I made up my mind to go there and visit the real thing.

Ah, San Francisco! In 1978 it looked so fresh to me. So many different kinds of people from everywhere. There was a spirit here I found enchanting. When you smiled at others they smiled back at you. And so many dogs. I knew this would be the place where nobody would force me to look at life a certain way, where I could be myself. Where I would someday like to die.

I have returned to my dreams now. To keep alive, my wife and I have started a Japanese language school. But I am also working to restore the Japanese cinema that has been dead for so long. I write for the movies now, creating stories of brave samurais to be played by American actors.

And every day I pray that the people of San Francisco will be happy."

Janice

"The very first time I brought Conor to meet my family, Mom was suspicious of him. And just to prove he wasn't looking for an easy way to stay in this country, she made him show her his green card. My mom's always been a perfectionist. While I was growing up, if I brought home a ninety-eight on a spelling test she'd say, 'How come you didn't get a hundred?' To her it wasn't enough that I be the best in everything. She wanted me to be perfect all the time…

Well, I'd met my husband-to-be in a sleazy place called The Mad Dog in the Fog on lower Haight Street. When he found out I was a dental student he came over from the bar to show me what somebody'd done to him at another drinking place the night before. There'd been a fight and they'd fractured off the lower edges of Conor's teeth with a pool cue. Would I fix them? I found myself instantly attracted to him, especially to that accent, and said yes.

Of course I knew from the beginning of our relationship that there were strong cultural differences between us. For example, on our first date at a Chinese restaurant he ordered chips with his curry. I thought he was kidding, but in Ireland, he said, they eat chips with everything. But in no time we became inseparable. Three months later he moved in with me at the dental school, and in November of '97 we became man and wife.

Life with Conor has taught me that I was completely naive in believing this marriage would approach perfection. The Irish way of living is to work really hard and play equally hard, and when you went out drinking you didn't stop 'til you were nearly puking your guts out. And Conor loves to drink and tell stories but doesn't know how to open up on a deeper level. He says life in America is very difficult, so if he has a problem he'll go out and have six or eight beers. But he's one of the best carpenters in the city, and I'm so proud when he tells me about all the compliments he receives. He has such a kind spirit, too. At least five times a day he tells me how much he loves me.

I've been practicing dentistry at the Western Dental Clinic for some time now, long enough to save up money to buy a house. We're moving to Moraga on the fifteenth of June. There's a lovely yard for Conor, Jr. to play in and Daddy's going to be putting on a new roof."

12

Conor

"Even if the economy was bad, I was happy and contented in Ireland. Sure, there was a chance of making a living in America, but the thought of leaving me native land was frightening to me. It was family pressure that brought me here. And the first couple years were tough, even harder than I'd expected. Not only was I plagued by homesickness, but good work wasn't easy to find. And I had the misfortune to be employed by some Irish contractors who didn't mind taking advantage of me. It was common practice – and still is – to use and abuse people like me who came right off the plane. Me own race exploited me and ripped me off, not caring that I had rent to pay. If it wasn't for meeting Janice and developing a relationship, I'm sure things would've gotten a lot worse for me. She was an Asian woman and such a contrast to what I was used to. Me mates urged me to go out with other girls – it was the American way, they said – but I thought that was a weird custom, and I told Janice it was her I wanted and only her.

We've had our ups and downs, like other marriages. Where I come from, the man is the dominant partner in the relationship – financially, mentally and physically. So here I am with an Asian woman born in a country with better chances of getting on, who's had a better education than me and is making more money. But Janice always told me she knew I could be successful because I'm bright, and I'm very grateful for her encouragement. What's also helped is I just completed a course in anger management at U.C.S.F. I always had a bad temper and a tendency to explode (which is an Irish trait), but I'm in much better touch with me inner self now. It's really helped me with Janice and with moving on in the business world. Here am I, the lead carpenter for a big company now, getting paid vacations and full benefits and making good money compared to three years ago. And last week I went out and spent four grand on tools to set me self up in me own business.

I doubt very much if I'd fit in any more in Ireland. I've become too Americanized and used to the way we live here. But, still, a piece of me heart is there, and there are times when I start to remember all the little things, like...seeing me brother and his kids, walking in the park with me dog...sitting on the front stoop with me mother..."

14

Suzanne

"

I always tell my sweetie not to worry about my safety and that I have absolutely no fear. There've been moments in my life, I'll admit, when I've been afraid, like that night on the beach in South Africa, where I come from, when a boy started messing with me. Oh yes, I was chilled with fear then. But rather than show it, I played games with him. I took my plastic eyes out and put them in my mouth, stuff like that – just to freak him out. I toyed with him for about an hour, 'til he got bored and ran away. But here in San Francisco, I'm pretty fearless.

It's the sighted people who are the fearful ones, and that's sad because fear can get in the way of living your life and expressing yourself. Life should be an adventure, so if I feel like going on an excursion, please don't anybody remind me that I might fall. I hate words like 'trip' or 'fall' or 'handicapped.' People look at me and think, 'Oh, isn't she nice. I wonder who dresses her?' They'll do anything for you because they want to have power over you. And, they'll get mad when you say, 'No, thanks, I don't need any help.'

I know I sound arrogant, and I realize people want to perform an act of kindness – and sometimes I let them help me for their own sake – but blind people should let people know how much they're capable of doing for themselves. I rode everywhere on my tricycle when I was little. And I climbed trees and jumped and walked wherever I wanted. In fact, I'd go out with the other little kids and climb the mountain near where we lived...

When people ask me how long I've been blind I tell them, 'What's the difference?' The visual thing is so strong with them. It's where they get most of their input, so they believe anybody who can't see must be hampered. Of course, you are in some ways. There's the feeling sometimes of absolutely no stimulation. It's so boring – a blank feeling in front of you. It hurts not to be able to see the sky. And what makes things worse are the hideous sounds in the city, and the smells, too, this city has very bad breath in many places – putrid, disgusting smells – it makes me wonder what they put in the world under us… But there are many sides to life, so many beautiful things, and I like to go looking for them.

I'm free to go wherever I like, so I'll spend three months here in San Francisco and three months in South Africa and three months in Scandinavia, and soon I'll be visiting my sister in Israel. But first, on the eleventh of May, I'm going to a Leonard Cohen conference in Montreal with my sweetie. And after that to Connecticut to visit his daddy…

I t's quite easy getting around by yourself. You pick up landmarks if you want to know where you are. Like an iron gate that makes a noise at my feet just before I come to an Indian shop I especially enjoy. Or the smells of incense and spices and things from a clothing store I visit. Once I heard a boy say, 'She really can see! Just look at her – she sees all the things around her!' But that's because when I'm near objects I can hear their outline. It's not that they make a sound. Things can be completely silent and I can still hear them. Like

there's a wall next to us right now, as we speak. I don't know how to explain it. Like yesterday, when my sweetie and I went on our tandem bicycle, I could feel the automobiles parked all along Golden Gate Park. And I kept telling him where the cars were and where they ended. I would go, 'Another one…another one! It's as though they cast a shadow on my field of audible vision. It's an incredible thing that you develop. And that's why I don't walk into walls and my face isn't squashed or anything like that. I can hear the openings in walls…the doorways… I can hear the difference between a car or a tree or a hedge. And I know just where to turn when I reach a street corner.

I lost my mom last year. She was run over by a car in Capetown. I used to neglect my mom and dad, but I learned a very hard lesson when she died. Her death was such a violent one. And so lonely. At the scene of the accident she lay there and said, 'I have nobody.' They wanted to know if there was anybody they could call and she'd say, 'There's nobody.' Kept repeating that. She died anonymous. She was in house of bodies before my brother found her. It was a dreadful experience, and I think it was her way, on some level, of paying us back for neglect. I always ask people, 'Do you have a mom and dad?' And without trying to preach, I say, 'Always look after your mom and dad.'

If anyone should ask my occupation I'll say I'm a street singer. Very often I'll take a bus to the farmer's market and sing for hours and hours. It can get extremely hot there in summer and equally cold in the winter. And when I'm tired, I drag my guitar, my amplifier and my bag back to 16th Street where my sweetie lives. It's very heavy, so I like to be strong. Amazingly strong. I try to be that...

There are so many things to do in the city... We ride our tandem bike all the way to Golden Gate Park and see all the flowers, and then we go to the ocean and ride along the beach. We go quite far and sometimes to parts where there's almost nobody else... And I love going to restaurants or to a coffee house and enjoying the communal feeling of people being together... Some days I meet my swimming buddies at the Dolphin Club by the Hyde Street Pier. We swim year-round, including winter when the temperature's gone down to forty-six degrees. We meet in the west room that overlooks the bay, where the view is so beautiful, and sit and discuss all the issues and questions of the day and of course we're inclined to laugh a lot. Sometimes they'll take me into the men's sauna and, just to be naughty, I'll pretend like I can see everything. Or we'll go to the gym and work out. And when we've had enough of that we walk slowly down the Filbert Street steps to the water. There's a man in our group whom I'm especially fond of. They call him Buddha because he has this big, big tummy! The first thing we do when we meet is bang on our tummies. When he's in the water he starts to sing, and he has this fantastic loud voice that you hear echoing through the bay. And we yelp and whoop and scream and make all kinds of noises. People are always telling us, 'Hey, you guys are having too much fun!' "

My dad stole a million dollars from the Mexican Mafia when I was little and then split to Spain. The mob thought my mom had the money, so when they put a hit man on her she flew from Mexico to Texas and turned herself in for felonies she was wanted for. After she got out, she took up with a guy named Greg who'd owned a dance hall in New Orleans and used to run a headshop in the basement of a church. Mom and Greg bought an old school bus, took the seats out, put in a sink, a stove and some beds, and we traveled through twenty-two states in six years. Me, Greg, my mom, and my four brothers and sisters. Plus some cats, dogs, mice and guinea pigs.

We explored the forests, cooked over campfires, swam, climbed trees and waterfalls, panned for silver and scoured beaches for abalone. Greg used to say these were our glory days. But when I turned twelve I woke up in the middle of the night and found his hands on places they shouldn't have been. I told my mom, but she said I was lying and was just trying to make her break off with him. And when he wouldn't stop I really started to hate him.

Mom and Greg did a lot of fraudulent things I can't tell you about because they'd have to go to jail if anybody found out. I was part of it, too. They taught me to be a con artist. I used to hustle money from relatives by telling them about our so-called desperate situation. But I wouldn't actually ask for the money. A good con artist studies people, looks for their weaknesses and plays them. Like I volunteered for the San Francisco Christmas Drive and told everybody how bad off my family was and they gave us thousands of dollars.

Then everything got really terrible for us. Except for the welfare checks Mom and Greg were collecting, I was the only one bringing home any money. And they were always telling me to go fetch stuff and wouldn't let me go to sleep. So one day I ran away and spent six months on the street. I'm in a foster home now. Greg's in the hospital dying. My brothers and sisters have been taken away by Child Protective Services. And Mom's in a broken down bus that's gonna get towed any day.

I've fallen in love with somebody and just got engaged. His name's Kenny and he's a Navajo Indian. I like him because he respects me and doesn't ask for anything. He just wants my company and that's it. I know because I've always been a cool judge of character. After all, I was raised to play people. And you can't play a player."

Bernard

"The American Psychiatric Association, in the early Sixties, was telling everybody what I did was pathological. But if I sought help, they said, I could be cured. And so, at great expense, I went for therapy. First I did Freudian. Then I tried Jungian. And I even found some meshugenah in Marin whose specialty was Reichian. He instructed me to take off my clothes, while he took off his, and we sat in a room and looked at each other for an hour and didn't talk.

I had been brought up an Orthodox Jew in Chicago, where I attended the yeshiva and went to synagogue regularly. My father dreamed that one day I would become a rabbi. Instead, I moved to San Francisco and became a stockbroker. But Judaism still had a strong hold on me, and I attended services at a conservative synagogue on Geary and Fillmore, where they kept asking me to come up to the pulpit and read from the Torah. This was causing me a lot of anxiety, and so one day I decided to pay a visit to the rabbi in his study and seek counsel.

'Rabbi,' I said, 'I've come to see you because I cannot reconcile coming to the synagogue, touching the Torah and being gay. Please tell me what to do.' The rabbi thought about it for a moment and said, 'Well, if I were you…on Thursday nights our Young Adults Group meets, so you'll come and find a nice Jewish girl and you'll settle down and…that's it…' 'But Rabbi, I don't think you understand. I am a homosexual. And you know what Leviticus says: Thou shall not lie down with mankind as with womankind. It says I'm an abomination! Rabbi, for God's sake, tell me what to do!' And he answered, 'Well, if it was me, I'd come on Thursday to the Young Adults Group, where you'll meet a nice Jewish girl and…'

After that I didn't go near a synagogue for a long time. The hell with it. But then one day I made up my mind to start my own synagogue. A gay/lesbian synagogue. And, in so doing, I broke with five thousand years of tradition. When Herb Caen of the San Francisco Chronicle found out about it, he wrote, 'Oh my God, my friend Bernard Pechter has started a gay synagogue! Now we have everything!'

It gives me great pleasure to announce that on the twenty-eighth of March I will be celebrating the fiftieth anniversary of my bar mitzvah at the beautiful new synagogue I helped found on Sixteenth Street and Dolores."

24

"The deal was we didn't have to have sex with the clients. Or even touch them. All we had to do was humiliate them. What a way to make cash, huh? Besides that, I was really fascinated by the culture. I could even shoot a documentary while I was doing it. Get an inside scoop. So when Ernest said, 'You have to come be my partner because you would go over so big in the bondage community,' I said yes.

It was really fun getting all dressed up. I had the same shoe size as Ernest and could wear his. They were thigh-high patent leather boots with six inch heels, and I'd lace 'em up and walk around like a giant Barbie doll, feeling really sexy – an Amazon bitch who could kick ass. And Ernest would show me all his equipment or even whip me and say, like, 'This is what I do.' He'd spent hundreds of dollars on leather gear, and he'd have this little dentist's tray in our dungeon with all his instruments on it. Dildos and condoms and all that stuff. And there was this creepy little photo on the wall of a baby in an old-fashioned dress and weird plastic fruit and kitschy mementos from the Fifties. And a giant pet cage with a black lace shawl around it. Most of the clients, as Ernest would describe them, were middle to younger-aged white-collar corporate execs who have a lot of power and who find the only way to get off is if somebody powers them. And maybe they're married and their wives aren't very experimental, or maybe they're single and they just can't find any girlfriends to do that.

Well, Ernest started telling me I had to buy this and I had to buy that, and I didn't want to put any money into it. I hadn't even had a client yet. And I wasn't really into it on a personal level. I just wanted to make money. I mean it was fun – I could even do it with my boyfriend, if he wanted it – but it really wasn't a lifestyle for me. And it got boring after a while: We'd sit around the dungeon all day and all night, too. It'd be dark with the curtains drawn. We'd talk and smoke cigarettes, and when the phone rang, Ernest would be, like, 'Hello, what's your name? What are you into? And what would you like me to do to you? Uh huh, uh huh...' And ninety percent of the time nobody would show. And then I began to fear being alone with a stranger I was doing bizarre things with. I just know my luck. I'd end up getting some crazy.

So I went out and got a job in an Italian restaurant instead."

Paul

"I was never able to ask them for money. How could I burden them like that when I knew how hard they worked? So from the time I was a little kid I cleaned yards, sold apples from our tree, walked little old ladies' dogs and shined shoes along Mission Street. There was plenty of time left over, though, for bikes, Cowboys and Indians and other stuff like baseball at Holly Park, the roller coaster at Playland and spooky movies at the Capri.

My friends in Bernal Heights were Latinos like myself, blacks and Italians mostly, and the offspring of people without much time for family life. We'd play in the streets from sun-up 'til evening. We loved to tease one another. If a kid was fat we picked on him. If he cried too much we called him a whiner. If he snitched we called him a squealer. But we always made up...

My mother was a happy woman who always tried to give us the best of herself. She worked as a maid at the Hilton Hotel for twenty-three years. My father was a quiet man with a taste for tequila. For a while I resented him: So many times I wanted to tell him, 'Just show me some time for a change! Give me a little attention!' But as I grew older I began to realize that he loved me and tried his best, so I stopped judging him...

When I grew up and bought my first used car, I was so proud, I said to my mother, 'Hey Mom, why don't we go to Mexico?' And that's what we did. We visited our whole family. But on the way back we stopped in Mexicali, where it was 117 degrees, and my mom got very sick. She was a diabetic, and when she stepped out of the car and into the heat she fell into a coma. A local doctor said her blood sugar was low and her blood pressure was high. He gave her insulin and said she'd be fine, but an hour later she died in my arms...

When I was twenty-seven, I met a woman from El Salvador who I knew was very special the first moment I looked at her. Something in her eyes told me she would become my wife. That's what she is. We have two kids now and are very much in love...

I've worked at Walgreens for nineteen years now. What I especially enjoy about the job is getting to know the customers. You share a lot of stories with them, some sad and some happy. You watch the young ones grow up and others getting older and unable to take care of themselves. So you try to help them. I tell them, 'Here, I'll give you my work number. Call me if you need any groceries, and I'll drop them off during my lunch hour.' And when I bring them, sometimes they'll have a sandwich and a bowl of soup waiting for me. You take care of them and they want to take care of you."

Maia

"My mom has eyes the color of blueberries, and they used to call her 'Blueberry Ike,' after a comic strip character of the time. She came from a very Norwegian family. Her grandfather wrote books about being an immigrant in America and of being a pioneer in the West. To this day we celebrate a Norwegian Christmas and eat lutefish, a horrible tasting fish preserved in lye. And when I was little she held me on her lap, called me 'Pumpkin' and read stories of Norwegian myth, all about trolls and elves and little creatures who lived under toadstools.

She never had that mothering, babying instinct though. She was never the kind of mom who ran around clucking like a hen or plumping your pillow when you were sick. We were poor when I was small, and it was of no consequence to her that my brothers and I didn't have toys like the other kids. At Christmas time we got books and socks. She believed that we could make something out of our imagination to play with. She didn't put my hair in braids or buy pretty dresses for me. I got hand-me-downs from my brother. And she did not like it when I took too much interest in my appearance. She believed there were better ways to spend my time, better pursuits than looking pretty.

I remember how terrified I was my first day of school and how she just put me out there. I'd never been in a situation before where I couldn't reach my mom. But I wanted desperately to show her I was brave enough to do this, so I just sucked it up and held back the tears...

She got married at nineteen and had her first kid at twenty, so she's never been able to do a lot of things in her life she'd have liked to. I don't mean to look down on her, but I don't want that for me. There's so much of the world I want to explore, and I can't live without my freedom and independence... I had surgery not long ago, and it was well after dark before I came out of the operating room. I woke up in the middle of the night with nothing but pain, feeling raw and unable to breathe. She was there, sitting on the floor next to me, awake, her head leaning against my bed, just resting there. Everything was okay then. I was a kid again. My mom was there."

Brother David

"My mother had two daughters by my uncle while my father was in the state mental institution. My uncle was a short guy with a mean temper and he was constantly beating her when he got drunk. I made up my mind that I was going to get this guy when I grew up. So when I turned thirteen I went to the corner grocery store, bought a bottle of wine, got my uncle drunk, invited him down to the basement and beat him half to death with a BB gun handle. And when he woke up, he realized he'd either have to stop beating my mother or take a chance getting whupped by me again.

I grew up in the toughest ghetto in Detroit, Michigan. It was so bad in the early Fifties, a gang of black guys and girls took over the high school. The principal called the police on the phone and said, 'The Shakers have taken over and are robbing everybody.' And the police answered, 'Call us when they leave.' My sister was the leader of the girl Shakers. My brother, at seventeen, whupped four cops in front of our house. And all of my father's children suffered nervous breakdowns.

My mom was high yellow with freckles and had a color problem. She treated her lighter skinned children better than her darker skinned ones. She never kissed me and never said she loved me. I was constantly giving her money and never got anything in return. When I was in the state mental institution she let a gang use our home as a safe house for stolen goods, but I put an end to that when I got out. Then the gang was after me, so I got Mom to move to the West Side.

Our new landlord didn't have any sons, adopted me at first sight and said he'd teach me the concrete masonry business. He took me around the city, showed me the porches he'd built on these gorgeous homes, and when he brought me back, gave me five one-dollar bills. That was 1957 and they'd be worth, like, fifty bucks today. Mom wanted some of it. I said, 'Okay, but let me just carry it around for a little while.' Mom went through a fit. Then I said something smart and she reached up and slapped me. And then she flinched. That's because the doctor told her not to whup my brother anymore after he broke his teacher's jaw. She was afraid since I'd been in the nuthouse I'd do the same to her. That's why she flinched. I looked at her, walked downtown, joined the Marine Corps and left that night."

Clare

"It's the summers back in Ireland I remember best – all sunny and fresh and new...standing in the kitchen with my mum while she pulled her big comb through my thick, curly hair. There were times when I thought she'd take my head off. After the ordeal was over, I'd run out to the street, swing around the lamppost and think up ways of doing mischief. My brothers and sisters and I adored a good fight – it was us and sometimes the Mooneys against the entire neighborhood. We got a big kick out of stealing the license plates off cars too, and, best of all, raiding Mrs. Moore's caravan. We knew her to be a witch because she had long, scraggly hair and a big nose. We were scared to death of her, so we'd run up to her property and play there and make a lot of noise 'til she came running out and chased us.

My dad was a fisherman and he used to take me out on his little cabin cruiser. We'd go all along the River Shannon and stop when we felt like it to visit all the different towns. And sometimes we'd fish off Dublin. Not anymore, though. My dad's mostly given up his fishing because the water's not very good, so these days he pretty much brings tourists out to the Irish Sea.

My mum was always very beautiful. In fact, everybody said she looked like Audrey Hepburn. I'd hear other girls giving out about their mums being strict and making them say their prayers and all that stuff, but I didn't have any of that with my mum. She never instilled anything in me. She let me discover for myself. 'And don't worry about the nuns,' she'd say. 'Don't be listening to what they say about God and that sort of thing – they're just people.' Like they used to tell us there was no sex before marriage. I believed it when I first got out of junior high – I thought it was this wicked thing – and then I just kind of looked around and figured out it's all a crock of shit.

All the time I was growing up, there were bombings going on up in the North. You'd hear on the radio that a bomb went off and that people were killed, and that was sad and awful. But you learned to switch off, you know. You'd bitch about the government and the English, but when you came down to it, you were powerless and so you'd switch off. After all, you were just a kid."

36

"Both of my parents migrated to the States and never forgot what their roots were. And I grew up knowing two different sides of the story; there's the old ways and there's the contemporary ways. Most of us try our best to fit in, but I probably wasn't very good at that because I had to do some fighting in school. There were a lot of gangs in the neighborhood and I fought because I didn't want to be part of what they stood for. I didn't feel a kinship to it. Theirs is not real Chicano pride.

Knowing your roots and your heritage is what Chicano pride is about, regardless of what everybody else is telling you... People have a picture of Mexicans that's different from what I've experienced. They think of bullfights and a guy wearing a sombrero crouched down on the floor with a cactus behind him and a bottle of tequila in his hand. But that's not what we're about. The real Mexico is a very strong indigenous culture with much to be proud about. We're a people who've persevered culturally, ethnically and racially and made it through a really tough part of American history. We've come a long way from the old towns and cities and the pyramids...

In my early years I tried very hard to find myself and see where I fit in. And sometimes I didn't like my brown skin very much and wasn't proud of who I was. Then I came to realize that your culture and heritage and how you look can sometimes get in the way. So I started looking deep within myself and discovered I was much more than who I thought I was...

My father'd had a very tough time growing up. His father had been a raging alcoholic and his mother died when she was thirty-five, so my dad had to support his little brother and sister when he was ten years old. He came from an entirely different perspective in life than I do. I was influenced by my brothers, who are artists and musicians, and I've always wanted so badly to create things and do something with my art. But my father told me not to waste my time. 'Do something that puts food on the table,' he always said. So over the years there was a lot of yelling and screaming going on in my house. Until one day I'd had enough and complained to him that in order to be worthy of him I felt I always had to prove myself. And I let him know how miserable he made me when I wasn't able to talk to him. He looked surprised when I said that and I think I might've hurt him. 'But that's all I ever wanted,' he said to me, 'to be able to teach...and be a good father and have peace with my boys. And love and respect in the house.' "

38

Margaret

"I wore overalls in the fourth grade and played football with the boys and most people didn't know what to make of me. I was in love with a boy named Matt McClure and followed him everywhere he went. One day I got up the guts to ask him if he'd be my boyfriend, and he crinkled up his nose and said, 'You're not a girl. You're a tomboy.' I was defeated and began to realize something was wrong with me... I let my hair grow out in the seventh grade, not that I preferred long hair, but because I needed some kind of validation that I was attractive...

My family moved to a different city, one where nobody knew I'd been a tomboy, and, as the years went by, I dated lots of boys... But when I was sixteen a woman kissed me and I stuck to the ceiling. And I thought in horror, 'Oh my God, I am that different kid. All this time I've been lying and pretending to fit in, but, in truth, I am this huge homo.' That just ruined my plans completely...

In my last year of high school my dad kicked me out of the house, and as I walked out the door he called me a 'pervert.' To resurrect myself from that has been my biggest challenge in life. Through the years, whenever I'd fall in love with somebody, I'd feel, on a deep level, that I didn't deserve love or an intimate relationship with anybody because I was a pervert. And one day the rare chance to speak the truth to my father came up: I'd just ended a relationship with a woman so beautiful even he liked her, and he said to me, 'How'd you screw that up?' On the telephone I told him, 'I loved you – that's why we broke up. Because my daddy called me a pervert and I couldn't even open my legs anymore – that was the problem!' I pleaded with him not to interrupt me, and he listened while I screamed and hollered, and he didn't butt in once. I thought he was a great man for that, and I think that's when I started to forgive him...and when I finally began to forgive myself for being who I am.

By chance, I saw Matt McClure one more time in my life. I had long blonde hair now, had lost the glasses and was wearing a dress because it was Christmas Eve. There he was, a bell-ringer in the Methodist bell-ringing choir. When the services ended I walked up to him and said, 'Are you Matt McClure?' And he looked at me and at my dress and kinda looked me up and down and said, 'Do I know you?' And I said, 'Yeah, you know me. I'm Margaret Sweeny. You wouldn't be my boyfriend in the fourth grade.' His jaw dropped a little, and I smiled at him politely and walked off."

He used to take me to people's homes during the late Forties to collect weapons that had been brought back from the war as souvenirs. Then we'd go to a secret loft in New Haven, where we'd watch women sew guns into linings of coats and jackets to be sent to Palestine. 'But, Dad,' I'd ask, 'isn't this against the law?' 'It's not a matter of law,' he'd answer. 'In another year or so, a Jewish state will be born and they will need weapons.' I remember the day we drove to New York and heard David Ben-Gurion build the audience to a frenzy. Franco of Spain had just agreed to allow Jews to walk through his country on their way to Israel. But he was demanding a thousand dollars a head. In a half hour that day they raised seven million dollars, and Dad and the others went back to their communities and raised more money.

Before coming to this country, my father and his family lived in a Polish ghetto under Russian rule. And while his brothers prayed, he crawled through sewer pipes and brought back bread and milk he'd stolen. That's how they survived before they made it out and settled in New Britain, Connecticut. His whole life's purpose was to save Jewish lives. And when my mother complained that he was getting too involved, he would go nuts. 'How could I not get involved?' he'd say. 'These are Jews.'

But he alienated a lot of people with his methods of collecting money. They didn't like it when he told them how much to give. And at the synagogue, where he was an officer, some of them got very angry when he said, 'If you don't pay, you don't pray.' I was petrified of him. And when I got older, we didn't get along so well. 'The macher,' he'd call me. Yiddish for 'big shot.' It rubbed me the wrong way when he spoke of us Jews as the Chosen People. And sometimes, when I argued too hard, he'd throw me out of the house.

He was in and out of hospitals in his later years. I was in California when they called me back. He wasn't the same man. There was something pent up inside him. One night he pushed me aside and, naked, went raging outside into the snow. I saw him for the last time at the state mental hospital. He looked at me and grunted, 'The macher.' Soon after that he died."

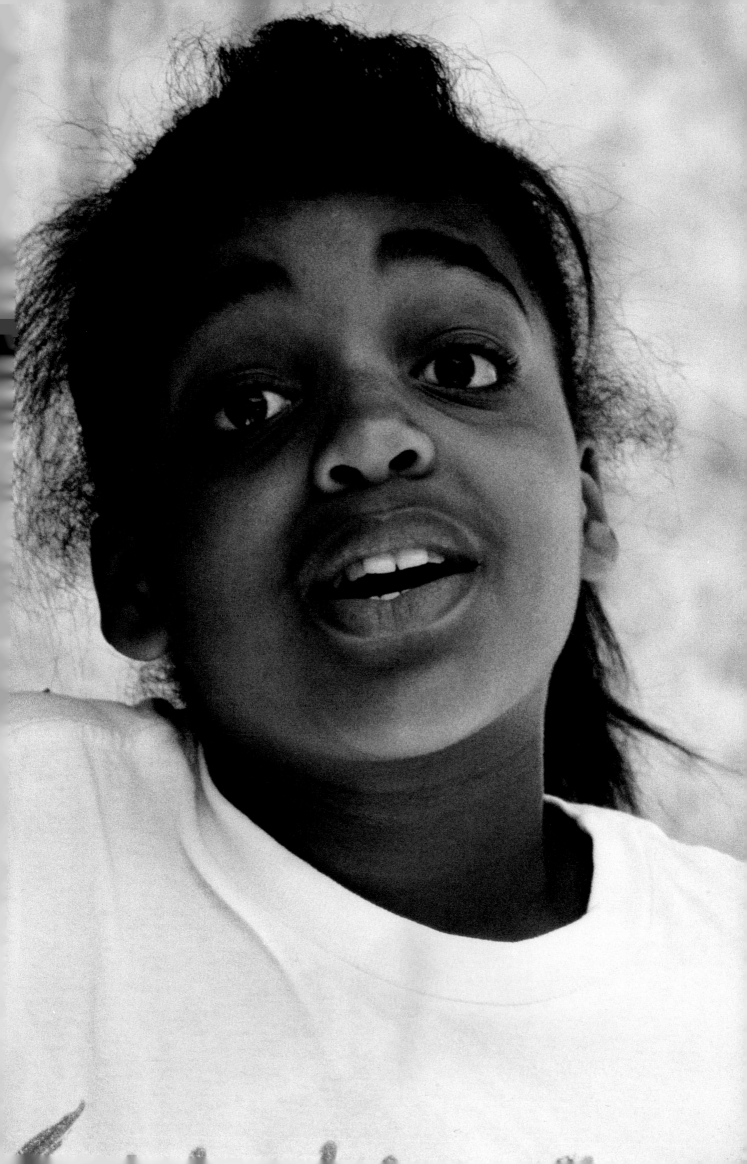

Joel

"A Mexican drug dealer with a tear drop tattoo next to his eye was looking for me in Seattle. He knew I'd ripped him off, and he was offering money on the street to anybody who'd tell where I was. That's when I decided to go to San Francisco, the junkie's land of milk and honey, where heroin was cheap and readily available. I told my parents I'd landed a carpentry gig someplace and hooked up with a kid named Kevin, who I didn't trust and had done jail time, but he'd been to San Francisco before and said he'd show me the ropes.

It was dark and scary when we got off the BART escalator at 16th and Mission and we were both strung out. There was sixty bucks between us and Kevin was holding the money. I began to suspect he was stealing from me when we copped and he made me stand in the distance while he made the transaction. But I was nauseous and my eyes were watery and we shot up right under a street light. Not long after that, Kevin got very abusive, and I ran off and hid in a doorway while he walked around yelling my name and saying he was sorry. But I fell asleep right there in the doorway and woke up a couple hours later starting to feel the magnitude of the experience. Here I was on the streets, in some strange city, with nowhere to go and totally alone.

But I met a lot of people like myself in the days ahead, all of them willing to do whatever was necessary to support their habits and stay alive. There were those who scammed the kids who came to the Haight on weekends to buy pot or LSD. Others stole from Walgreens or Safeway and brought the stuff to the donut shop on Mission and 20th, where they'd post a sign, 'Do Not Try To Sell Items Here.' But the truth was they'd buy cigarette cartons, colored crayons, videos, ladies' underwear or just about anything you brought them.

Thanksgiving morning I woke up completely broke in a dark garage some place. I was experiencing the beginnings of withdrawal, so I went to the check cashing place on Valencia Street, called my stepfather and cried to him that I needed money to get on the methadone program. I was lying sick and helpless on the bench when the money arrived two hours later. Some of the guys, who'd long since burned up their own resources, were waiting with me. I felt a new surge of energy as I bounded down the street for my fix. The others came with me. And by nightfall all the money was gone."

46

Scott

"I couldn't get her to understand what a dangerous game she was playing. I bought her everything from pepper spray to Siren Scream. I even taught her how to use a weapon, but, man, I couldn't give it to her. The first time I did, she got it taken away and damned near lost her life then. My biggest fear was her being attacked and assaulted and dying out there.

We had a fight the last time I spoke with her. 'Yeah,' I said, 'you can come and get your clothes! Whatever the hell you want!' Slammed the phone down and went to work. Came back later and no evidence whatsoever of her coming around. Tuesday night came and went. And Wednesday, too. Thanksgiving morning I leave the hotel to get a cup of coffee and Homicide shows up while I'm gone. When I come back, somebody says, 'I'm really sorry to hear about Shellie.' And I go, 'What are you talking about?' 'Oh, man, Shellie was found dead this morning.'

I'd lived without a partner for fourteen years before I met Shellie. It was a loneliness I could control and had learned to live with. Years before, after the death of my son, I saw the whole world in shades of black, white and gray. Everywhere I looked there was death. And if a car went by with an empty baby seat in it, I would start breaking down and crying. If I smelled baby powder, I would break down. If I was in the company of others, I would have to bite a hole in my lip. But when I coupled up with Shellie, I felt like there was a purpose in my life. Even in getting up at four-thirty every morning and knocking my head against the wall as a carpenter.

One day I picked up a paper and read they arrested this guy who assaulted a nineteen-year-old girl with a hammer, rolled her up in plastic and threw her off a dock. A block from where they found Shellie. I know he's the guy who murdered Shellie. I found his name in her little book. But the D.A. says he'll only get eighteen years and be out in nine. And he's only fifty-two, so he'll live to do this all over again. My mind starts running tapes, like I know enough people in Folsom and San Quentin who'll take care of his problems. But that's not my job in this life.

I can only live with the hope that it'll get better for me, her son and mother and father and all the friends she had and didn't know about. The whole town showed up for the funeral, God bless her. She was a wonderful soul. We'll never know the real Shellie."

A short guy walked up to me on the street in the early Nineties and said, 'Hey, baby, how you doing?' I'd just come here from Texas and was being exposed to this intense radical dyke consciousness. And I was bald-headed and working in a dyke bar and very sensitive to somebody calling me 'baby' or 'sweetheart' and all the other sexually demeaning ways you're put down on the street. So, like a warrior, I stopped and said, 'I'm not your baby, little boy – little teeny weenie.' And he starts yelling at me and calls me 'bitch.' I'd surprised him when I didn't smile or walk by him and feel intimidated. Instead, I was like, 'Hell hath no fury like a woman scorned.' In those days I was angry all the time, especially when I walked by those insulting billboards and when I saw how couples reacted to me. I was suffering from a victim thing that I had to work through. There were dykes I knew back then who wouldn't go out with me because I didn't hate men. They were total lesbian separatists then, and today many of these same women are dating men.

So the little guy called me 'bitch' and I'm, like, 'No, you're a bitch.' And he told me with an attitude like mine I was going to get popped some day. And I said. 'Well, pop me! Pop me right now then! I'd rather die right here and now than kiss your ass and be afraid!' Then he turned and walked away, and a second later I heard a forty-ouncer whizz past my head, barely missing me. I was pretty shaken up by it, but felt good that I'd stood up for myself.

But when I got home, I thought about who I'd had this battle with. Some young Latino guy, barely able to speak English, hanging around the streets of San Francisco. And I'm thinking, who am I fighting here and where does most of the oppression of women come from in the world? Is it from this guy in particular? And how does he perceive me? Maybe to him I looked privileged. So here we are, both fighting a common enemy, which happens to be the unfairness in the world. We've both got some things to be mad about, but is yelling and screaming the best way to deal with them? Or did I have to, like, build a life for myself and not get angry with people?"

Scott

"Every summer my hometown was invaded by artists and writers and a lot of fun, creative people, and in a week Provincetown would change from a sleepy little New England fishing village into this completely mad scene with lots of enthusiasm and a really high energy. So, as a kid growing up, I felt like I was raised in two different towns at the same time and had the benefits of both. I knew fishermen's kids and Norman Mailer's children and Eugene O'Neill's descendants, as well as the offspring of people nobody ever heard of.

It was a town of infinite variety, and my family fit right in, my dad being an artist and my mother, a teacher. Dad was this wild hippie from the Bronx who did portraits and caricatures of people in the streets. Summers he would have the tourist trade to make his money and in the winter he would paint, which is what he really loved to do. My mother, who'd been raised in a strict Lutheran community in rural Pennsylvania and was a go-getter and a well-organized professional, taught at the local high school and ran her crafts shop in the summertime.

I met so many different kinds of people – artists, writers, fishermen, teachers, hippies, squares, gay, straight, whatever – in that town, every way of living seemed acceptable. And my mother and father were loving folks who treated my sister and me like equals, were always supportive and never pushed us in any direction, so we enjoyed the luxury of being able to experiment with ideas and figure out what we wanted to do with our lives. And I had the belief I could do anything I wanted to.

But I think it was our town doctor who inspired me to choose a career in medicine. He'd go out to the boats and help the fishermen get their fingers out of machines, take care of all the old folks in the nursing home, put people in their graves and of course he'd been there to deliver almost all of us. He always looked tired from working seven days a week, and half the time he'd get paid in the form of lobsters and paintings.

But they all helped me become who and what I am. They taught me to go out of my way to make human contact with my patients, see them eye to eye and know that what happens between us is important. It's not a matter of another number on an H.M.O.'s register. Or another dollar in the health care system. It's a real person. And maybe I've played a part in making his life better."

Jean Marie

"He was very good looking, spoke Spanish and had that Latin charm. That's all I remember about him. He abandoned us when I was six years old. He hurt my mom so badly she never went with another man again. I think she still misses him to this day. She gave me a lot of love, though, became my best friend and instilled in me the drive to go on. But I always yearned to know more about my heritage, especially after Mom, who is not Mexican, introduced me to my dad's father, who was living in Arizona. Grampa spoke no English, kept a Chihuahua in a cage, grew chili peppers in his backyard and slept with a crucifix over his bed. Meeting him was when I made up my mind to see Mexico.

I was twenty years old when I got there and took a job in Puerto Vallarta. Wherever you went there was music playing: You snapped your fingers and in a moment someone would be serenading you. You went to a party and the grandfather would sing a song and the children would join in because the songs were handed down from generation to generation. Little kids played on the sidewalks with just sticks and cans and were perfectly contented, while the grandparents sat close by in rocking chairs and watched them. There were no convalescent homes there – people took responsibility for their elders until they died. They lived in cement houses with dirt floors, kept them immaculate and lived happily for the rest of their lives. Their doors were always open – you walked by them and you saw the people inside eating and talking... The family was everything... I would have stayed forever in that country if I could've. But the immigration authorities picked me up and tried to kick me out. Then the economy got so bad I was down to just one meal a day and starving.

I came back to America and took a job at Walgreens in San Francisco. That's where I met the man who would become my husband. He was a Latino and very charming. He brought a trio to my house and serenaded me. We went together for a year, grew to love each other and got married. Our wedding was the happiest day of my life. I gave him two daughters and, at long last, had the family I always wanted. But seven years into the marriage he told me he was moving out. Then he went to live with a woman a block and a half away. I couldn't believe he abandoned me with these two girls."

Bob

"When a letter arrived for me back in May of 1967, I thought it was my income tax refund. But when I tore it open, it said, 'Greetings. You are now a member of the United States Armed Forces.' I thought, 'What the hell's going on?' I was home from teacher's college for the summer and was supposed to be exempt. Everybody said, 'You'd better go down to the Selective Service Center and straighten it out.' So that's what I did. The recruiter there was a master sergeant from the Air Force, who told me, 'Listen, with your background and intelligence you better try and get into the Air Force because, otherwise, your ass is gonna get stuck in the Army, Navy or Marines.' So I took his advice and was able to get in. They gave me six weeks of basic training and then assigned me to the Strategic Air Command in Florida. I got so hooked on what they told me there that I volunteered to go to Vietnam and was sent to a top secret Air Force base. And I never saw any part of these United States again, except when my mother passed away and, five years later, when the Red Cross wrote that my father had suffered a fatal heart attack.

If you didn't experience that tragic period of our life, you would never believe it. And if you were there, even today you probably would not believe it. I was involved in top secret, covert missions connected to the CIA and flying arms to mercenaries all over Cambodia, Laos and Thailand. On one particular mission I was ordered to perform what they called 'justified murder and mayhem.' And they told us that after we finished the job they would be back to pick us up. But they knew what we were doing was out-and-out war crimes and so they just left us there. That way nobody would be alive to say what was being done and by who. I ended up in a P.O.W. camp for fourteen months and, but not for some friends, I'd still be there.

Some three hundred and fifty thousand of us have died since that war was over with, and up until a year and a half ago they wouldn't even recognize that I have Agent Orange. Because that's three hundred and fifty thousand claims they didn't want to fess up to.

Every day, when I say my prayers, I ask myself, 'What the hell was going on back then? What the hell happened?' "

56

Apacuar

"I was born in Bethel, the main village of the Yupi'k tribe, which is located right above the Aleutians and along the Bering Sea. It's very flat there, mostly tundra, with lots of lakes, rivers and swamps, but no trees. To this day there are no roads leading to and from my village. The only way you can get there is by using a small aircraft, weather permitting in winter. Long before the white man actually set foot in my village, a shaman was able to describe with total accuracy what the boat would look like. And while I was growing up I heard many stories about how frightened the villagers were when he finally did come.

One of my first memories in this life is of a tribal dance in which I took part. I was two years old when I got up from my mother's lap and turned into an animal.

It is the custom of my community that you carry the spirit of the person you are named after. I was named after my father's father. He died before I was born, but I've gotten to know the kind of person he was by the way people always treated me. One year there was a long, harsh winter, and for a while people in the village weren't able to find any game. My grandfather saved everyone from starvation by catching a seal and giving it to the community. When people tell me that story, I feel very honored to have acquired his name. I was raised with the values that I'm expected to help other people, regardless of who they are. What I say or do will not only reflect on me as a Yupi'k person but on my family and my community. I keep that in mind in whatever I do and whenever I come across something that is presented from the outside world.

I made up my mind while I grew into manhood that I would go off to different place, get a good education and then return to my people and give back what I could to the community. After I graduated from the University of Fairbanks, a program was started in Alaska that addressed the native gay men. There were six of us who were asked to join a focus group, and, in so doing, provide personal experiences and ideas on how to reduce the number of people who will get infected from the H.I.V. virus. My job now is to travel the country providing technical assistance, first and foremost, to native people. It's work that I have no trouble committing myself to because in my community alone there's now a high number of teen pregnancies, people who are incarcerated and substance abuse. In a village of four hundred people, all it takes is one person to spread the disease and a whole community can be wiped out."

60

I bore five babies by my first husband in four years, but when I realized he wasn't going to give me the white picket fence I wanted, I left him. I saw real estate as the way to my picket fence, so I took the state exams, failed them, took them again and failed again and passed in the third attempt. I learned how to work smart when I started selling houses, but what took me many years to discover was you don't make money speculating real estate.

I met a bartender and dated him for many years before getting married again. He was good to the children is why I married him though, not out of love. He didn't drink until he married me and then he just drank and drank. The outcome was he developed a liver problem, diabetes and a brain tumor, and he died. By then the children were grown up, and one thing I instilled in them was when you turn eighteen I'm not going to baby-sit you anymore. I'll see that you go to Catholic schools and get a good basic education, but when you graduate I'm done with you.

I never thought about what life would be for me without children. I never could figure out what I wanted to be or do. So, for the time being, I just lost myself in real estate. I took the brokerage exam in Virginia and turned my twelve-room house into a home office. It all looked good on paper and everything seemed to be in order, but I started losing and going down. By 1980 I decided to retire, sell everything I owned – except what I could put on my back – and leave the country.

I loved being in far away places with different languages, attitudes and approaches to life. It allowed me the freedom of not having to identify with anyone. Over there you sat on a rock and looked at the water, saw a fish and got in the water with it. You waved to someone on a yacht going by, and the next thing you knew you were on the boat with them. And you didn't even know them. I met a man from Australia, much my junior, and we had a romance on this huge ship sailing around the Grecian Isles. He had a cabin and I had a cabin, but we ended up on deck with our sleeping bags. Sleeping out there under the stars."

Saira

"I sleep in the same room with my sister Monica and I've noticed that sometimes she goes to bed without saying her prayers. I tell her, 'You should pray, Monica.' But she doesn't listen and goes right to sleep. I pray every night. I pray in Spanish. I don't know how to pray in English that much. I pray for the drunken man who sits on the steps of the empty house next door. I pray for all the poor people. I feel so bad when I see them in the streets. I pray for the people who die, too. My grandfather died when I was in first grade. He had something inside him. I think it was beer that killed him. I'm never going to drink or smoke when I grow up.

My mom and dad love me very much. They teach me to dance and take me shopping and buy me shoes and movies and 'Hello, Kitty' things. And help me with my homework. I love going to school. Yesterday I was in a talent show. I sang Christina Aguilera's song, 'What a Girl Wants.' A lot of other people sang it too, but when I'm singing or dancing I feel the music. And I feel my heart saying, 'You should do what's right.' "

Before I was born, my father was a sergeant in the United States Army Air Corps and a big war hero. After the Japanese attacked Corregidor in '42, he survived the Death March, escaped a prison camp and became a spy for the Allies. Being a Filipino and knowing his way around the Islands, he would gather information about the enemy's gun emplacements, deliberately get himself captured to find out more and then escape time and again.

He married my mother after the war and in the Sixties they had me. But it didn't work out. Every night he would come home and start yelling at everybody. Finally, she took me to the airport and said we were leaving and never coming back. All those years I was with her I lived in a total state of grace. She was a real mom – took me bowling and to the movies, turned me on to the Beatles. Then one day my father appeared out of the blue and took me away. I never saw her again. And it had been so long since I'd been with him, it was like living with a total stranger. Even when I grew older I wasn't able to connect with him. If he wanted me to do something, I did the opposite. He tried to groom me to be like him, but my world was hanging out with the counter culture and the Grateful Dead or going to Alaska and being on my own on my motorcycle.

I was having dinner with him in '94 when he suddenly passed out. I couldn't revive him, so I called the ambulance and they diagnosed it as a stroke. After that, it was a downhill scenario. His brain had been damaged severely and there were liver problems and, later, he had a heart attack. He died on Veterans Day.

In the cemetery, while we were burying him, there were all these veterans hanging around. I gathered them together and had them salute while my father's body was lowered into the ground. It was my way of respecting him as an old soldier."

"My mom and dad met at a bus stop in San Francisco and got married in a little chapel on Mission Street. She was part Mexican, Scottish and English, and Dad was a Filipino, with a little Irish and Danish blood mixed in. I was always this blonde kid. We lived in the projects at Hunters Point and were so poor I used to steal the milk bottles off the neighbors' porches. But when I got a little older, my grandmother let me work on her ranch in Geyserville. I drove the tractor, picked fruit and aerated the soil.

One of my happiest memories of those times was when I watched hundreds of people walk by, all shouting and singing and led by one man: 'That's Cesar Chavez,' Grandmother said. 'He's marching all the way to Eureka to help the farm workers.' She used to hide all the illegal immigrants in her house, and when the authorities came to look for them, she'd send me outside to pretend I was playing. And they'd see this blonde kid and turn around and leave…

By the time I was full grown I knew I wanted to become a professional artist, especially after I won a prize in the ninth grade for my ceramics. But I was still hounded by poverty and not eating too well. One day I heard about a big art show coming up, and I had some nice pottery but nothing to fire it up with. That's when I came up with the idea of borrowing some car paint and using it on the pottery. When somebody saw it they said, 'Hey, that's really cool! Can you paint my motorcycle tanks?' 'Sure,' I told him, 'I'll be happy to.' And when another guy asked me to paint his VW bug, I said to myself, 'Hey, I can make some money doing this – I'll have to put my art aside for awhile!'

So then I joined the Air Force to learn the body shop trade and, when I got out, opened my own place. My first year I made $39,000, and a few years later I bought the big shop I'm operating now. It's a great business, with fifteen employees and a twenty-year lease, so I'll be here awhile. But I'm in love with art as much as ever: We're putting in a little ceramics studio upstairs, with a kiln and a line for glass blowing. And I'm always hiring down-and-out artists to paint murals on the outside of my building. It's the only body shop in the city with murals – maybe in the whole world!"

"My father didn't like me much because I came out different from what he'd expected. He was hoping for somebody with straight hair and fair skin like my mother. He used to lock me in the closet for hours. When I was two years old, he locked my sister and me in the apartment and went out drinking. The building caught fire and somebody carried us down the fire escape. It was dark and there was nobody to look after us, so I was standing outside crying when my mother came home from her night job. That's when she decided to leave him, which didn't bother me much because I knew he beat her and I once saw him throw her out a window.

Then she married a white man, and he took us to live in Irvington, New Jersey, which was predominantly Jewish at the time. They didn't integrate much in those days, so we were the only blacks in our building. People used to drive by and look at us, and the kids in school called us schvartzes. I was afraid to go there. In fact, I goofed off a lot with my life when I was young. I didn't take anything serious. I just wanted to run around, you know, go to Woodstock.

But all that changed after I grew up and moved to San Francisco. And I wanted to make sure my daughter was everything I never was. The person I had her with didn't want to marry me. That's how it is with some men. It's easier for them to walk away. I felt bad for my daughter that she never had the security of her father. I never asked him for anything. 'You don't have to support her,' I told him. 'Just be there for her.' But he lived his life and took his skiing trips to Aspen and abandoned her. I cleaned apartments six days a week, my daughter worked from the time she was sixteen, we stretched our meals and she graduated out of Mills College.

I used to be a smoker and didn't get much exercise until the Eighties. Then I started running. I found a track next to a school building and started working out there. One day a teacher came out and told me he'd been watching for a year. 'It's time to fly away now,' he said. 'Let's see how far you can go.' I ran all the way to the Bay Bridge and back. So I was a runner now and started entering races. It's fit my life perfectly since my daughter's gone and I don't have any family anymore.

Life's been like a school to me. And I believe we all know what the lesson's about before it ends. I try to live right and show kindness to others. We're all connected in this universe, and the path has to do with forgiveness and an unconditional state of mind towards others."

Tracy

"It became the most beautiful place on earth every autumn. On the mountainsides were miles and miles of blueberries, and all these flowers and gorgeous rocks. My dad would take me out of school sometimes and we'd go hiking and fishing in those mountains. Sometimes I'd go up alone. I was a tomboy in those days, and I tried to prove to myself I wasn't afraid of anything. I'd just throw on a backpack, grab the dog and hike all the way up to the ridge. I could see the clouds moving in over me up there. And I'd pick blueberries, sit and eat my lunch (and get my butt all stained with purple spots) and watch the dog jumping and chasing squirrels and rabbits in the tundra. That whole part of Alaska's bear country, so I'd kinda be looking around, and I'd always carry a forty-four-caliber pistol with me. Bears are pretty to watch, but you never know what they're going to do, and you don't want to become somebody's dinner.

I grew up with a couple of awesome guys who'd bend over backwards to do anything for you. We used to go swimming and rapid-romping together. In the fall, when the water started to get ice on it, we'd strip down to our underwear and go swimming and come back and warm ourselves by a big bonfire. When we became seniors in high school, and our class went abroad for Spring Break, we hung out in Europe together. And from the time we got off the plane we took not one sober breath… after all, we were seniors – we had no choice. We'd hit the pubs all night and the churches and museums during the day. Europe was a blast – it's where I grew to love art and history.

After high school I got a job in a gold mine. I'd work a few months, save some money and go someplace I'd never been to before. Someday I hope to travel all over the world – even if I have to go by myself. There's one thing life has taught me, and that's to be secure within yourself and not be afraid to be alone. San Francisco's just another stop in my journey. This is my favorite city I've ever lived in. I love my apartment. I love my boyfriend. I love my best friend, Katie. I'm working for a construction company. None of the other girls from the temp agency wanted the job. I love being able to see something built out of the ground. We completely renovated an old historical building this year, and already there are people living in it. It's the most awesome thing to watch people moving into something you've been working on for a long time."

Julio

"There was this contest in school, right? They told us to listen to a song they played and draw something to it. I drew a picture about people trying to make you into something you're not. They just drive you crazy – so crazy you don't even know who you are any more, you know? The people in my picture wore straight jackets and were made out of metal. And I won the contest.

Drawing is very important to me. I don't ever draw pictures of stick figures and kid stuff like that. I draw ideas and dreams. My teacher says I have a very good drawing perspective. Sometimes she gets me in front of the class to demonstrate to the other kids. I like to do that.

One time I drew how the sun reflected in the mirror. I'd seen that once, and so I just closed my eyes, remembered it and drew it. My drawings are kind of complicated. When people ask what they mean I tell them I don't know. That's because what I see in my vision I just draw, that's all. I can't explain it – it just comes out, comes off my pencil.

I've always been a very competitive person. My dad taught me to be that way. He doesn't want me to do some lowly job when I get older. He wants me to go to college and grow up to be somebody. He says I can do anything I like with my life, but I must always do the right thing at the right time. But I don't really like being competitive all the time. If you're in first place all the time, a lot of people will want to knock you down. But if you're in last place, there's nowhere to go but up."

Jeffery

"My first client was a man who lived in a little house in Diamond Heights. I gave him baths, took him to the toilet and sat with him on the porch and read him books and magazines. He was so unbelievably nice. Much of the time he needed to lie naked on the living room floor by the window so the sun could heal his bedsores.

There were times, as I sat there watching him, that I wondered what my mother would say if she could see me now. She'd been a New York socialite and my father was a wealthy lawyer. I had all the advantages while growing up – horses, dancing school where everybody wore white gloves, summers in East Hampton, boarding schools and college in Massachusetts. But except for a daughter by a man I divorced, my life didn't amount to much until I started my volunteer work.

One day, when he'd gotten worse and was frightened and unable to keep any food down, he looked at me and said in a quiet voice, 'Do you think we should say a little prayer?' I said, 'Of course,' and he recited the prayer and I said, 'Amen.' It was the closest moment I ever had with him.

A few days later his companion called me in the middle of the night and asked me to come over. I'd had no idea my friend was so close to death."

I was very frightened when the doctor told me I had colon cancer, and I certainly wasn't looking forward to the surgery he was going to perform on me. Then I thought about it awhile and called upon God for His help. After all, it's His world, isn't it? He brought us here, and if He wants He can take us away and find something better for us. There's nobody's getting off this place alive.

There was a time when I didn't know what my life's purpose was or what I was striving for. And then one day three brothers, all dressed in white, opened the door of the cab I was driving and said, 'Are you ready to become a Muslim?' I said I was, and they took me to a mosque, where I took the oath, 'There is but one God and Muhammed is His Messenger/Prophet.' I've prayed five times a day ever since, and that's taken care of the spiritual aspect of my life. I may have slipped now and then, but that's all part of being a Muslim: Taking a step backward and a couple forward, regaining and continuing on.

After the operation, the next thing I did was book passage to Mecca. There were millions of us there, all performing the same ritual. And when I walked by the shrine of the Holy Prophet Muhammed I could feel His presence. It was as though He was alive. I was so moved the tears flowed from my eyes.

We're all on a journey and going back to God. And being a Muslim is wanting for everybody what you want for yourself, whether it be a house, a loaf of bread or peace of mind. I had grown up in Harlem, New York, where my family was among the first to live in the projects. In my early days I used to stand on the corner with my friends and beg quarters to buy beer. But times have changed for me. I have a nice job, a beautiful wife and family and I'm nurturing a good spirit by worshipping the Creator in a prescribed manner. Bowing my head five times a day.

I've always loved working with the public, and for the past sixteen years I've been driving a Muni bus in San Francisco. It's nice, you know, getting the people home safe. If you've taken my bus, you've heard me singing. My father's sister used to perform in the Cotton Club, so I guess it's in my blood. And when you have a song in your heart you just want to give it to the world."

Robert

"I'd just been to the bank to cash my first paycheck in awhile and had stopped off at a smoke shop to buy a fistful of cigars, when I heard the voice of a saloon call my name. 'Ro—bert,' it said, 'it's really hot out! Come in and have a nice cold beer!' But I didn't pay any attention to the saloon. I'll put it off 'til tomorrow. And when tomorrow comes, I'll put it off 'til the next day. And the next day. And the next. Putting off saloons for one more day is what I've been doing for fifteen years now. One more day. One more day. It doesn't mean I've been a great human being for fifteen years. I haven't been hanging out in Calcutta saving lepers with my sidekick Mother Theresa. But at least I haven't been getting picked up for vagrancy or drunkenness in public anymore or being a social pain in the ass. In that respect I've done my part for world peace.

Instead of going to the bar I went to one of those fruit juice stands on Second and Market, ordered a Virgin Pina Colada and sat there smoking my cigar, sipping a cool drink, watching the street cars go by, feasting on the hustle and bustle of the city and checking out all those stunning women. Especially this six-foot, buxom Nordic blonde. Plus I had a couple shekels in my pocket and the satisfaction that went with it. I felt like the cat that ate the canary. And I wondered if Jack Nicholson was having as good a day.

If you're an alcoholic like me, you'll do anything to keep the _____ty alive. Until one day you're either dead or, on a very deep level, you know the horror must stop. I will go to any length to prevent the past from happening again. No matter what my circumstances. Seven miles in the snow without shoes. To any length. To any length.

But whether you're drunk or sober, life keeps showing up at your doorstep. And for all the toil and sweat and bullshit we go through, there is also sipping a fruit juice and smoking a cigar and watching people on a beautiful afternoon. And loving my girlfriend, Christine. And sitting in the bleachers with the other dads and moms and watching my son play Little League when he's having a good game. Or getting up on a Saturday morning and making breakfast for my children. Frozen waffles with fresh strawberries, swimming in butter and Canadian maple syrup. The kids think they've died and gone to Sugar Heaven.

When it's good, it's good. And when it's not, it's okay."

Imet him at a birthday party for a mutual friend. He stood in the corner watching the people and appeared very quiet and lonely. It took all my courage and the apple schnapps I'd been drinking to ask him to dance. At first he said no, he didn't know how. But I talked him into it and we did very well together. A week later he was at my house for tea and we began seeing each other regularly. I had no idea he would become the man of my life. We were both only fifteen years old. And I hadn't any idea yet who I was or how I wanted to live my life.

But we soon learned that we shared a love for travel. In those days we were two young romantics, and for our first big trip we chose Verona, Italy, where Romeo and Juliet had lived. When we arrived there with our tent and backpacks we looked for a nice green park to sleep in. But what we found was loaded with criminals, and so, instead, we returned to the railroad station and slept there."

We had lived in that same little town near Cologne, Germany, all our young lives, yet we'd never met until the night of that party. I was really surprised when she came over to ask me to dance. She was so beautiful. I have always considered myself fortunate that I got to know her at such an early age. And that we have been able to share so much of our lives together.

In those early years I was working for my father in his small factory. And then he got sick and suffered terribly. Chris stood by my side all through those years. And so now we've been together a long time. It has changed a lot because we have come to know each other so well. We've both learned that to grow and achieve serenity it's important to go our separate ways sometimes. And yet often it's still like a honeymoon."

"We were fugitives of the Idi Amin government in Uganda and living in New York where my father was attending Columbia University. But every summer he'd take us to Vermont where we lived in a beautiful red house on the shores of Lake Champlain – Mom and Dad, my two little sisters and me. At dinnertime we'd walk down to the lake house and eat with all the relatives, the grown-ups at their table and we kids at ours. It was the perfect life. Waking up in the morning and swimming in the lake. Ice cream after dinner. Playing games with my cousin. And having stories read to me.

Sunday evenings were the best time. A neighbor would put stereo speakers on the dock and play classical music. He always began with Bach's 'Jesus, Joy of Man's Desiring.' We'd paddle our canoes out on the lake, lie perfectly still, listen to the music and watch the sun go down. Or sometimes my grandmother, who I especially loved, would bring blankets and quilts, wrap me tight, and we'd sit together in a big wicker chair and hear the music from the porch.

My father wasn't with us our final summer at the lake. He was in Michigan where he'd gotten a teaching job, and we were to join him later. My mother's father had just died in Uganda, but she didn't dare go back for the funeral, for fear of losing her life. Then one Sunday morning after church, when she and I were walking down the road past the white picket fence that surrounded our beautiful red house, we saw the ambulance take my grandmother away. That was the final ending to all our Vermont summers.

Dad came down for the funeral and to take us to our new world in Michigan. My mother sat in the car the entire trip without speaking. But what I remember best is my dad's crying. He just cried and cried and cried. Until then I had always believed that grown-ups had some mysterious power that informed them of just what needed to be done and how. But not now, not anymore. Now they were these fragile people. And I wasn't sitting at the little kids' table anymore."

Jack

"When you weigh two pounds at birth, grow up short and have to fight your way to the synagogue for Hebrew lessons, you acquire a chip on your shoulder. And, boy, did I have a chip. I was an angry, restless kid. King of the hooky players. I used to throw water bags on priests from rooftops. I had my first experience with a woman when I was twelve. Third guy in line in a gang bang.

There are hiding places in my room
where beautiful poems are hidden

Poems hidden away in boxes
on sheets of brown paper

Poems of spirit and magic...

I knew way back that I was special. I just didn't know how to tap into it. So I lived in this fantasy land. It's the only way to take this world because it's just too cruel. I asked a rabbi once, 'Why is it the rich people who buy a ticket for the High Holy Days get to sit in the front and the poor people have to sit in the back?' 'Because that's how it is,' the rabbi answers. He told my mother I didn't respect the rich and would have trouble every day of my life. He was right, too.

There is a crazed eye of a poet
in my room

There is the sunlit morning

There are dancers dancing in my room

There are old Arabs exploring
the desert near Escalon

There are sparrows and bluebirds
and wildcats in my room

There are elephants and tigers
and skinny Italian girls in my room...

I don't know what went wrong in my life. How come I don't have a telephone? Why am I a recluse? How come they look at my shoes when I walk in an art gallery? You like these shoes? I bought them from a guy on Mission and 18th.

There are the steps of Odessa
in my room

There are the Pictures of an Exhibition
in my room...

I ran into a guy once who knew me from the old days in New York, when my name was Harvey Silver. He'd seen my picture in a book called 'The Beats'...

Mussorgsky and Shostakovich
and Charlie Mingus in my room

Composers and painters
all singing in my room

All hidden away in boxes...

'...All of a sudden Harvey Silver becomes Jack Micheline,' he says to me. He thought it was miraculous that I'd popped up with a brand new name and was published with some of the great writers of our time.

One night when the moon is full

They will all come out and do a dance."

90

I was going with a boy at Stanford and we were getting ready to be engaged. But I was having a lot of fears and conflicts because my religion said I couldn't marry someone who was not Christian. But by that time I had already given him my heart. And so I said to God, 'Father God, if You don't want me to be with this person, then You will have to change his heart. Because my heart cannot be changed.' The very next day the young man said to me that, for some reason, he'd begun to realize he didn't love me anymore and that it was better for me to go my separate way. It was the shock of my life to have an answer to prayer that quickly, and it was very painful, too.

I was at a loss as to what to do and how something so devastating could turn into something good. All through that process I think God was trying to teach me how He wanted something better for me. Then I started hearing in my heart God telling me to worship and celebrate Him and to do it through dance. I had studied ballet as a child but gave it up at sixteen because in Kentucky, where I was living, Baptists don't dance. But now I knew I had to start all over again.

Then it happened that a woman at Stanford was looking for someone to dance in the Easter celebration for Resurrection Sunday. It was an invitation to come out and worship God and be healed and to do it in the context of a community that was celebrating the resurrection of Christ and the resurrection of a new life.

And so I began to see the possibility of dancing in a way I never thought about before. I had always believed that dancing was about beauty and technical perfection and passionate artistry on stage. And being a star. But now I was learning that there's something about dance that is powerful when it is done in longing to know the God who made you and the God who heals you and the God who calls you by your new name.

In the spring I will be inviting my family and close friends and church family to a dance piece I'm working on, in which somebody turns to God in the midst of pain and darkness. It will be about sacrifice and loss of innocence and repentance. And how the presence of God transforms pain into something beautiful."

My father wanted me to be a carpenter like himself. But I didn't want to be no carpenter. I was always in love with engines. I dreamed of walking into a Boeing 167 and repairing it. To work on an airplane engine – that's something, isn't it? If I can live a little bit longer, I might still have a chance.

When I finished high school and wanted to join the Army, my mother begged me not to go. I was her only child and she knew they'd send me to Vietnam. But I said I didn't mind going to Vietnam, wasn't this what I was supposed to do? Part of growing up in this country? Other people went, didn't they? Why shouldn't I? 'Don't go,' she said. 'Don't go. Don't go. Don't go.' So I went. Not too bad for a while. But then it got worse.

When I got hurt, they repaired my leg and put it all back together again. But the ankle hurt really bad. Worse, I developed an addiction to Percodan for a couple, three years like you would not believe. Had to have it every day. Had to have it. Had to have it. Had to have it. I slept all the time when I took the pills, but then the pain would wake me up and I needed to take more.

So one day I asked the doctor, 'Is it possible, Doc, this leg's going to repair so you can get me off these pills?' Doc said, 'Well, Edward, I'm going to answer your question: Repairing it's impossible. The pain's going to be there forever. That means you have to take some drugs for it or you won't be able to stand it. But you have an option. You can have it amputated, get off the drugs, walk down the street like everybody else and have bad dreams for the rest of your life about not having a leg. Now what you want?' I said, 'Doc, let me think about it for a while.' So this went on for another six, eight, ten months thinking about it, and I would take eight or nine of these a day, until finally I say, 'Doc, cut it…off! Cut the motherfucker off!' Hah hah hah! So he cut it off. And this thing here – you see me walk, huh? I walk like everybody else.

And when I dream, I dream I have two legs. Ain't never had a dream I have but one leg. Can you imagine that? Haw haw!"

He used to come to all my soccer games and was our one fan. He lived only five minutes from where I grew up and had gone through the same school system. All I knew about him was he was a really nice guy and four and a half years older than me. Then one night, when my sister gave a party for her friends and I was there just kinda hangin' out, he showed up.

'Are you still playing soccer?' he said. I felt a little awkward standing there talking to him. Why would he care about me? But then I noticed he wasn't looking over my shoulder at the people coming through the door. He was looking only at me and seemed really interested in what I had to say. We just talked the night away. Not long after that, he went off to college and for two years we carried on a long distance relationship. My mother and father liked him and let me visit him on weekends. Or he'd drive four hours down the California coast and we'd go for hikes or swim or bike ride or take trips to the desert. My favorite of all places was Laguna Beach where we had our first kiss. We'd sit on the rocks in the coves we loved, listen to the waves crashing around us and stare at the stars. Afterwards, we'd go into town, get an ice cream and walk on the boardwalk.

I was sixteen and Steve was twenty-one, and he had friends, lots of them, who said our relationship would never work. But he never told me that and never let on about all the teasing he took. Later on, when I found out, I realized it must've taken a lot of confidence on his part not to let it get to him. He loved me that much.

The day of our wedding I had to be up at five in the morning to get dressed and have my hair put up. My sister, who was the maid of honor, helped me... When the steam train carried us up the Santa Cruz Mountain there wasn't a single cloud in the sky. Sis and I sat in the last car, and we were so excited that every once in a while one of us would let out a little scream. On the mountaintop, a woman played Cat Stevens' 'Morning Has Broken' on the guitar, and in a clearing surrounded by redwood trees, my husband and I took our vows. And the morning light filtered through the trees and put a soft touch to everything."

Ike.

" When I came to San Francisco forty-two years ago, I'd tell my students to be as attentive as possible, learn as much as they could and have lots of fun. At the end of the day I wasn't giving them any homework. 'When that bell rings,' I said, 'it's over for all of us, teacher and students. Go out and expand your horizons.' I can't speak for them, but at 3:30 or 4:00 I was out for my afternoon walk and discovering how accessible nature was in this city. And if you look at the Pacific Ocean today or the bay or the hills of Marin, they're just the same as they were back then, despite all the social changes that afflict this city. To this day I'm amazed that I can get to the ocean in fifteen minutes. I look at those big waves and the birds and gaze up at the sky and forget every problem I ever had.

I really needed to be on my toes, of course, when I was in the classroom with the children. I'd been trained to make the day interesting for them so that they'd enjoy coming to school. And that's what I tried to do. Many of them had problems that weren't of their own doing – like the children of the Seventies who'd come from Central America and had been ravaged by the wars. They'd lived such unstable lives; some of them had never been in a classroom before. Others had such bad family problems it was a struggle for them just to graduate.

I always felt a sense of loss when the children moved on. You wondered what would happen to them. Will they be all right? Will they get in trouble? It's a heart-rending experience to know you can't work miracles with them. All you can do is plant a seed and hope that someday everything will work out...

But of course you do run into some of them eventually. I had the most wonderful experience yesterday: I was in the bank, and this girl walked up to me and said, 'Did you work in Everett Middle School?' I said yes, and she said, 'I was there. I graduated in 1992. I hope I was one of your good students.' I said, 'Dear, you're wonderful. You're wonderful now, you were wonderful then.' It's astonishing how mature and settled they become after you haven't seen them in ten years. But then, of course there are those who go to jail for drugs and whatnot. I'd be foolish to think that doesn't occur. But you wonder all the time about them: Where are those kids? Where did they go?

By the early Nineties, I started to slow down, grow weary and lack the energy level I used to have. I knew it was the aging process at work and that my body was wearing out. That's when they made me school librarian. Of course I tried to take it all in stride by sticking to the routines I was used to, as well as through my enjoyment of nature and meditation. But more and more I found myself thinking about the finiteness of human life. I've had some trouble with my eyes and skin cancer, but I feel okay. Not to the extent, though, that I don't anticipate the possibility of things going wrong, nor do I want to live to an age where I'm infirm and helpless. And, by the way, I believe in God – the God of all living things – not just the people who've been favored by special chances.

As I approach seventy years of age, I still take my walks, but I've cut back a little. I used to do ten miles and now I do four to six. I want to live a life that has validity apart from this whole modern insanity of television, Internet and computers. I've read a lot and written a twelve-hundred-page book of meditations based on the mystical traditions of East and West. And, of course, I always try to live in anticipation of human finiteness. A life in the schoolroom teaches you how things have a beginning, middle and an end. They come into your classroom and…suddenly it's over… They're gone from your life forever…

I've barely begun to learn how to live. I never wrote all the books I'd hoped to and haven't read a tenth of the fine collection I own. I've hardly traveled in my lifetime. I know people who've been all over the world by the time they're twenty. Been to India and Nepal, been here and there and the other place. I marvel at this. Maybe all these years I've enclosed myself in a more secure world than I should have by living in San Francisco. I probably should have been more daring and risk-taking. It's a feeling I've scarcely seen anything… Maybe I'll do one big major trip in this life… But I do hope that I have good karma and that I can go on to make further progress after it's over.

I look at the lives of people and believe that we're just beginning. I'm not talking about the human race going on to do incredible things in the next million years. I'm talking about the individual person. He is the beginning, middle and end of reality. He is the heart and core of everything."

Author's Page

I was fresh out of the Army, pushing twenty-four and sharing a small bedroom in my parents' house with my baby brother. I didn't know what to do with my life yet, which created tension between my father and me. So I escaped to New York, moved in with an Army buddy, signed up for an acting class in the Village and took a night job at NBC. It wasn't as dull as most jobs I'd had and was definitely more fun than the Army. They had me working "The Tonight Show" with Steve Allen and shuttling back and forth between Perry Como and "Tic Tac Dough." Then my father paid a suprise visit, checked out my page's uniform and said, "This isn't for you." He never liked it when I disappointed him, so I said I'd give NBC two weeks notice and study to be a teacher. Looking back on my life, I'm grateful for having been a coward and not standing up to an overbearing father. I think I was a young man who needed a nudge. My first teaching job was in a New Jersey high school. I'd sign in at 6:30 a.m. and, most of the time, not get home until dark. I was in charge of the drama program. We'd rehearse for months, play to packed houses and take our shows to drama festivals all over the state. It got me a college teaching job and a chance to work at the Bucks County Playhouse with actors I'd loved on the big movie screen. But it all came crashing down when the playhouse filed for bankruptcy, and when the college politics turned ugly, I resigned.

By now I was pushing forty-three and had a family to support. Luckily, somebody had built a shopping center in Morrisville, Pennsylvania – in it was a movie theater and nobody to operate it. So I signed a lease, took a crash course in theater management, borrowed money from the bank for theater equipment, advertised and opened for business. Our first features were "Cabaret" and "Snoopy Come Home." I loved the movie business, but I missed the creative activity of teaching and play production, and the camaraderie that went with it. Alone at night, after selling the nine o'clock and cleaning the popcorn machine, I felt the compulsion to document my life, so for nearly twenty years I wrote plays about a character named Movie Man. In the last of them, Movie Man bids goodbye to the neighborhood kids who'd been his customers; not one to hold grudges, he forgives them for carving up his seats and peppering the screen with Jujyfruits – he's exultant because he's moving to San Francisco. But, before he goes, there's one scene he must play. Seating himself at the ticket window, he awaits the inevitable appearance of his father's ghost. "You'll go broke in a month out there," the old man will yell. "You'll be forced to live in one of those awful hotels. In the middle of the night, desperately lonely and hungry for conversation, you'll invite your friends the cockroaches in and to them you'll describe the wreckage of your life." But Movie Man is ready for him and, at long last, knows that he will prevail.

I gave up playwriting in San Francisco and started taking pictures. They were mostly of people I saw in the streets. I would put them on the walls of a bagel shop, and people would come and look at themselves. Sometimes they brought their friends with them.

Once a lady walked up to me in the street and thanked me. She said one day she'd like to own a book with my pictures in it. I haven't seen her since – I don't even know if she's still in town – but, lady, if you should read this, thank you.

You too, Dad.

DayBue Publishing

*"An empowering work of art can illuminate the mind
and awaken the heart."*

Based in Sun Valley, Idaho, DayBue is an independent family-run Publishing house dedicated to publishing high quality literary fiction and nonfiction. As publishers, we look for undiscovered gems that we feel passionate about. DayBue is dedicated to quality and excellence and committed to integrity in each step of the publishing process. Rather than choosing to publish books of a certain genre, the most important criterion is that each book we publish is artfully and exceptionally written, with the potential to illuminate the mind and awaken the heart.

Visit our web site at www.daybue.com

Other Titles by DayBue Publishing

Church of the Dog by Kaya McLaren
184 pages
ISBN# 0-9668940-2-2
Fiction

Church of the Dog is "a rollicking, inviting, eccentric novel" (SARK, author of *Succulent Wild Woman*) that expresses a joie de vivre that touches the hearts of readers and invites them into a world of astonishing possibility. Mara is an unconventional spirit who brings her zest for life to Earl and Edith McRae and permanently alters their simple lives. In the tradition of Barbara Kingsolver's *Animal Dreams,* Kaya McLaren captures the intimate and complex emotions of life in small town America.

Language Lessons by Mary Clare Griffin
208 pages
ISBN# 0-9668940-1-4
Nonfiction / Memoir

Mary Clare Griffin was devastated when her mother was diagnosed with breast cancer. **Language Lessons** is a story of self-realization, her mother's struggle with the illness and how it brought a mother and daughter together and allowed Ms. Griffin to begin the healing process. "Mary Clare Griffin writes with grace and courage about estrangement, reconciliation and the ultimate survival of love." — Molly Giles, Pulitzer Prize nominee

Moonlight on the Ganga by Claire Krulikowski
192 pages
ISBN# 0-9668940-3-0
Nonfiction / Travel Memoir

Claire Krulikowski's vivid, inspiring prose takes readers to the sandy banks of the sacred Ganges river and through the ancient streets of Rishikesh on an eye-opening and soul-searching journey. Indulging in **Moonlight** is like taking your own journey to India and experiencing the mystical lure of the trembling, surging stream. The river serves as heartbeat and backdrop for the search for life's meaning. "***Moonlight on the Ganga*** is lush in imagery, bold in articulating experience and allows the reader to reflect on the spiritual essence of his or her own life." — Dr. Lauren Artress

Surrender by Stephen Burke
262 pages
ISBN# 0-9668940-0-6
Fiction

Eric Petris had his entire life planned out: successful lawyer, husband, father. A sudden epiphany alters the trajectory of the course that he has followed. Leaving his job, his house in the suburbs and searching for his life's true meaning, Eric Petris begins a quest for a new reality. *Sun Valley Magazine* raves "Once in a while, fervent readers get a chance to indulge in a book that changes the way we think and view our somewhat insignificant spot in this vast world. ***Surrender*** is that and more."